Library of Congress Cataloging-in-Publication Data

Henry-Biabaud, Chantal

  Living in The Heart of Africa

illustrated by Jean-Marie Poissenot; translated by Vicki Bogard

Translation of: Au Coeur de l'Afrique, le long du fleuve.

Includes index.

  Summary: Describes aspects of daily life along the Zaire River
in Central Africa.

1. Congo River — Desciption and travel — Juvenile literature

2. Congro River Region — Description and travel — Juv. Lit.

[1. Congo River — Description and travel. 2. River life. 3. Zaire —
Social Life and Customs.] I. Poissenot, Jean-Marie, ill. II. Title.

III. Series: Young Discovery Library; (Series): 29.   90-50774

DT639.H4713   1991   967.51   ISBN 0-944589-29-4

Printed and bound by L.E.G.O., Vicenza, Italy

CHILDRENS PRESS CHOICE

A Young Discovery Library title selected for educational distribution

ISBN 0-516-08292-2

Written by Chantal Henry-Biabaud
Illustrated by Jean-Marie Poissenot

Specialist Adviser:
M. Muka-Katombe
Cultural Attaché
Embassy of Zaire

ISBN 0-944589-29-4
First U.S. Publication 1991 by
Young Discovery Library
217 Main St. • Ossining, NY 10562

T 53061

967.51
HEN

YOUNG DISCOVERY LIBRARY

Living in The Heart of Africa

Kinshasa is
capital of
Zaire

6

All aboard for a trip up the river!

We leave from Kinshasa, capital of Zaire, in Central Africa. On the banks of the mighty Zaire River, modern buildings and mud-brick houses stand side by side.

Since dawn the port has been jammed with people in colorful dress, waiting to board the boat. A hot sun beats down. People in dugout canoes glide up and down the river, watching the hustle and bustle.

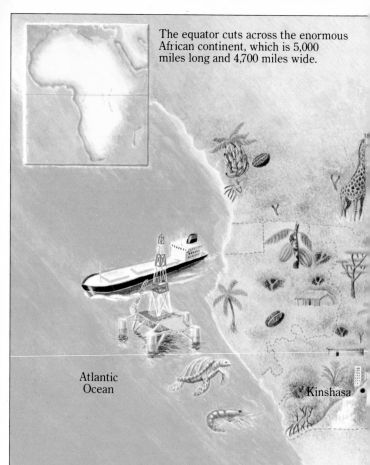

The equator cuts across the enormous African continent, which is 5,000 miles long and 4,700 miles wide.

Atlantic Ocean

Kinshasa

The Zaire River was once known as the Congo River. It forms a 2,900-mile-long arc which crosses the equator in two places. But the Zaire is only good for boats between Kinshasa and Kisangani, where it is as wide as nine miles in spots.

The rest of the river is too
dangerous for boats because of
waterfalls and wild rapids.

Mbandaka

Kisangani

In the desert, nomads are always moving
their herds in search of watering holes.

On the savanna, lions hide in the tall
grass and stalk antelope or giraffes.

In the tropical rain forest are tall
trees, vines, monkeys, and butterflies.

There are two main deserts in Africa:
The Sahara in the north and the Kalahari in the south. Not much rain falls, and little grows there.

agama

Closer to the equator, it rains more. **This is the Savanna**, or grasslands, where tall grasses and a few trees grow.

oryx

Very near the equator, when it rains, it pours! The air is hot and sticky, and the sky is often full of low, heavy clouds. This part of the country is covered by the great equatorial forest, **the tropical rain forest.**

gorilla

python

The boat is ready to leave! Two or three thousand people hurry on board with their pots and pans, sleeping mats and baskets of food; not to mention their chickens and goats!
Everyone rushes to find a comfortable spot: the trip will take a whole week, and there will only be a few stops.

everyone wants
to get on the
boat.

12

A long whistle blast and the last packages are tossed aboard. People who came to say goodbye now leave the boat. Sometimes, in all the shoving, someone or something falls into the water! Now it's anchors aweigh!

As the boat departs, the passengers make themselves at home. They unroll sleeping mats, cook dinner, play cards, and even dance to music from transistor radios. It is like a floating city with a captain for a mayor, heading slowly up the muddy river.

River traffic is heavy and the captain must be on the alert.
Watch out for those log rafts being floated downriver!

Look out for those sandbars! You never know where they will be—they keep shifting. And what about those pesky water plants that get tangled in the boat's propellers? Some of those plants were brought to Africa by Europeans. They grew too fast in this climate and now nobody can seem to get rid of them. The captain must think about the safety of his boat and his passengers at all times.

The okapi is a strange animal. It has the head of a giraffe, the body of a donkey, and the legs of a zebra.

Near Mbandaka, the halfway point of our trip, the forest gets thicker. There are towering mahogany trees whose wood is used for making furniture. There are palm trees and kapok trees whose pods are full of a fluff, like cotton, that we use to stuff pillows. In the tangle of vines hang other growing things, such as beautiful orchids and poisonous plants.

There are giant beetles, termites and army ants which can eat a whole person. And butterflies: the African giant swallowtail has a wingspan of up to 10 inches.
You might also get to see a rare animal which lives only in Zaire: the okapi.

Here's a village of huts with mud walls and thatched palm roofs. There are no roads or trains. Everyone travels on the river. When our boat arrives, it's a big event!

The villagers run to the shore
and wave. Some paddle their dugout
canoes close to the boat to sell
catfish or monkey and crocodile meat!

**Two important people in the village
are the chief and the witch doctor,**
who gets rid of evil spirits.
Everyone has a job to do.
The men cut down trees
and clear
the forest with
machetes. This
provides firewood
and space for new
huts and gardens.
They fish and go
hunting with
their little dogs
by their side.

The villagers work out their
problems under the "palaver
tree." Palaver means to discuss.

The women grow a root vegetable, called
manioc, in their gardens. They carry
large bundles of it in the heat. In
the village, the root is soaked for four
or five days before eating. The women
also fetch water and firewood, and
wash clothes in the river. Much of
the time they work with their babies
strapped to their backs.

Market day is a big event!

Early in the morning, when it is not too hot, the women come to buy and sell. They display their wares in baskets, basins, or on pieces of cloth spread on the ground. There are delicious fruits: mangoes, bananas, pineapples, papayas, oranges, limes, coconuts...

There are vegetables such as manioc, yams, or sweet potatoes.
They sell yards of brightly colored cloth to wrap around their bodies.
You can also buy fish or smoked crocodile, monkey meat, antelope, or elephant.
Care for a dried caterpillar?

Women skillfully carry enormous pots on their heads.

A calabash

**At an early age children
begin to help in the work.**
The girls, wearing hair braided
in many styles, help their mothers
pound the manioc. The manioc meal
is rolled into balls, wrapped
inside a big banana leaf, and
steamed over the fire. It is
eaten with a spicy sauce.
Boys learn to hunt and fish
by going out with their fathers.
They practice animal calls so
they can lure game into traps
or shoot it with arrows.
All of the children are taught
to respect their parents and
to help others in the village.

A village school
is a few benches,
a blackboard,
and the teacher!

What about school? Many villages
don't have one. Then the children
must walk for an hour or two to
another village. When they get home
in the evening they are often too
tired to finish their homework.
For high school they have to go
down river to a large town.

When the children have a little
free time, they make their own toys.

A good crop, a wedding, a new baby: all call for a celebration! The villagers put on carved wooden masks, feathers and animal skins. They paint their faces and bodies. Then they dance all night to the rhythm of drums. Every village has dances that show the courage of its warriors in battle and the defeat of their enemies.

Deep in the forest live the Pygmies.
They are a tribe of small people who do
not grow more than 4½ feet tall. They
were probably the first people to live
in Central Africa. The forest is their
home. They know
how to make their own
soap and toothpaste
out of the plants
that grow there.

Pygmies live in huts made of curved branches covered with big leaves. They catch animals and gather fruit in the forest. Roasted caterpillars are a favorite. Pygmies are skillful as dancers and musicians and they know what plants make good medicines. Every few months they move to a new area.

Hunters make poison-tipped arrows to stun game.

How do you catch a fish?

Some men fish from dugouts using rods with single hooks. (Often these fishermen gather to race each other.)

Others do not wait for the fish to come to them...they go to the fish!

This fisherman swims underwater and expertly spears his dinner.

And there are other ways to fish.
A few miles from Kisangani, the
last stop on our trip, the river is
full of waterfalls and rapids. Here
fishermen hang long baskets from
platforms. The platforms are made
by lashing tree trunks with vines.

Every so often, a fisherman will dive
into the water to check the baskets. If
there are any fish inside, they pull up
the baskets fast! Sometimes they catch a
giant two-hundred pound catfish.

If we leave the river and go down a dusty red road, we will arrive at Virunga National Park. The park has volcanos and lakes and something special. It is the only place in the world where you can see mountain gorillas in the wild.

On the shores of the lakes, there are thousands of birds. Pelicans with long beaks and baldheaded storks wait patiently, hoping for scraps from fishing boats. The catch is smoked and shipped to markets in town, or grilled and eaten right by the lake.

Virunga may be the most beautiful animal preserve in the world.
Elephants, water buffalo, antelope, lions, leopards and hippopotamuses all live there. They are protected, but illegal hunters, **poachers**, still try to kill these fine animals. Park rangers chase and arrest poachers.

On the outskirts of a village there are some tame animals. You can touch them but it still is funny to be nose to nose with an elephant! In the bush it is better to keep your distance...

Preoccupation

Dust is in my eye,
A crocodile has me by the leg,
A goat is in the garden,
A porcupine is cooking in the pot,
Meal is drying in the pounding rock,
The King has summoned me to court,
And I must go to the funeral of my
    mother-in-law:
In short, I am busy.

A Mbundu poem

Index

Books of Discovery for children five through ten...

Young Discovery Library is an international undertaking — the series is now published in nine countries. It is the world's first pocket encyclopedia for children, 120 titles will be published.

Each title in the series is an education on the subject covered: a collaboration among the author, the illustrator, an advisory group of elementary school teachers and an academic specialist on the subject.

The goal is to respond to the endless curiosity of children, to fascinate and educate.

For a catalog of other titles,
please write to: Young Discovery
P.O. Box 229
Ossining, NY 10562